Friday Night with the Pope

Jacques J.M. Shore

Illustrated by
Amalia Hoffman

Typesetting by S. Kim Glassman

ISBN: 965-229-370-9

Edition 1 3 5 7 9 8 6 4 2

Gefen Publishing House, Ltd.
6 Hatzvi Street
Jerusalem 94386, Israel
972-2-538-0247
orders@gefenpublishing.com

Gefen Books
600 Broadway
Lynbrook, NY 11563, USA
1-800-477-5257
orders@gefenpublishing.com

www.israelbooks.com

Printed in Israel   *Send for our free catalogue*

To His Holiness,
the late Pope John Paul II,

and

His Eminence
Cardinal Stanislaw Dziwisz

two most special friends
to whom I will forever be grateful
for their warmth and kindness

Foreword

The story you are about to read is true and tells of my experience with Pope John Paul II on a visit to the Holy Father at his Vatican residence in June 2003. While I was not the age of eleven-year-old Jacob, I wanted to share the story through the eyes of a boy because I felt that I was a child in the presence of the late pontiff. I also believed that children reading what happened during that Friday night Sabbath dinner would better understand the Pope's teachings as told to a child. With an understanding of these truths, it is my hope that children will be able to share the Pope's lessons so as to spread goodwill and build bridges among all people on Earth.

Jacob was full of excitement, for tonight he was in the beautiful city of Rome, Italy, on a visit to see the great Pope John Paul II.

While Jacob had met the Pope on many occasions, tonight was going to be a special visit unlike any other. For Jacob and his mother, Lena, were invited to the private home of the Pope to have a Shabbat dinner.

"Have you ever had a Shabbat meal with the Pope?" asked Jacob as he hopped and skipped through the cobblestoned city. "No, this is the first time," answered his mother. "I am just as excited as you are."

Jacob's mother always spoke about the Pope with great affection.

They had both grown up in Poland and she had known him for many years. "As a child, the Pope always helped others, regardless of religion."

"When the Pope was your age he loved playing sports. His team would be made up of Catholic and Jewish players," said Jacob's mother.

"He was friendly with many young Jewish classmates at a time when they were being very badly treated by others. This made the Pope sad because he believed that to hate anyone was wrong."

"Today he has made it his special mission to bring together Jews and Christians," said Lena.

"What did he do?" asked Jacob.

"He was the first Pope to officially visit a synagogue, Auschwitz and the State of Israel," replied his mother. "He has always believed that all people should be treated well."

As Lena and Jacob arrived at the Vatican where the Pope lived, they were reminded again that he was no regular person.

There were many gates to go through before reaching the
inner courtyard of the Vatican apartment where the Pope lived.

Entering St. Peter's Basilica, Jacob felt butterflies fluttering in his stomach. The Pope's residence was magnificent and grand, with marble floors, high ceilings, beautiful crystal chandeliers, and wonderful, large, colorful paintings.

All Jacob's nervous feelings were soon gone when he saw the Pope's warm smile. Jacob looked carefully at everything; he wanted to treasure this special moment.

Dressed in a long white robe and a white headcovering, the Pope seemed to be surrounded by holiness. Jacob felt good just being near him.

"Is it true your name used to be Karol before you became the Pope?" asked Jacob.

The Pope began to laugh, "Yes, it is true, my name was Karol Wojtyla."

"Why did you become a priest?" a curious Jacob continued.

The Pope took Jacob by the hand. "As a child I suffered terrible sadness and grief when my mother passed away. Just a few years later I experienced another loss, the passing of my brother. I was able to turn my sorrow into a mission in life to help others and always knew that it was my calling to serve God."

KAROL

Just then, Monsignor Dziwisz and Father Mietek, who were the Pope's special helpers and friends, greeted Jacob and Lena, and lead them to the dinner table.

Tonight promised to be a special evening – longtime friends celebrating the Shabbat together.

Entering the dining room, the Pope reached out to Jacob and Lena, giving them a broad and beautiful smile.

"Jacob, would you like to begin the *Kiddush?*" asked the Pope.

Jacob smiled and eagerly began the special Shabbat blessing.

"Blessed are You, God, our God, King of the universe,
Who creates the fruit of the vine," he said in Hebrew.

Jacob passed the *kiddush* cup of grape juice around the table and continued with the blessing over the bread. He picked up the bread that was placed on a gold and white plate and said the blessing:

"*Blessed are You, God, our God, King of the universe,*
Who brings forth bread from the earth."

As the meal was served, Lena and the Holy Father shared childhood memories. Jacob learned that the Pope had mastered eleven languages. He also learned that the Pope loved acting and poetry, and enjoyed going to church to pray.

John Paul II turned to Jacob and explained that a world that does not share love and kindness is a world that loses a day to help those less fortunate. "No matter what religion, ethnicity, skin color, or culture, we are all the children of God. God watches over us, but we too must take care of each other."

The Pope continued, "We witness the sun as it rises in the morning, we see it set at night, we marvel at the colors in the sky and then we grasp the vast beauty of the stars above. God gave us streams, oceans, valleys of green grass, trees, and mountains to climb. God gave us flowers to share with those we love. Our God would want us to take care of these first gifts he gave to us. We should be thankful for the beauty and we must do what we can to preserve and protect it."

The Pope placed his hands over Jacob's head. "Jacob, the spirit of Heaven is here – here on earth; we just need to find it and plant this spirit in our everyday life."

"Please remember this and tell your friends – so they too can tell others. On this Shabbat, we are sharing the spirit of love and friendship, things we all wish for. Heaven will touch the earth when we love our neighbors as ourselves."

Jacob whispered, "I promise."

After the Shabbat dinner, when it was time to leave, Jacob hugged the Pope and the Pope kissed Jacob on his forehead. They waved goodbye. Jacob and his mother thanked the Pope for allowing them to welcome Shabbat into his apartment in the Vatican.

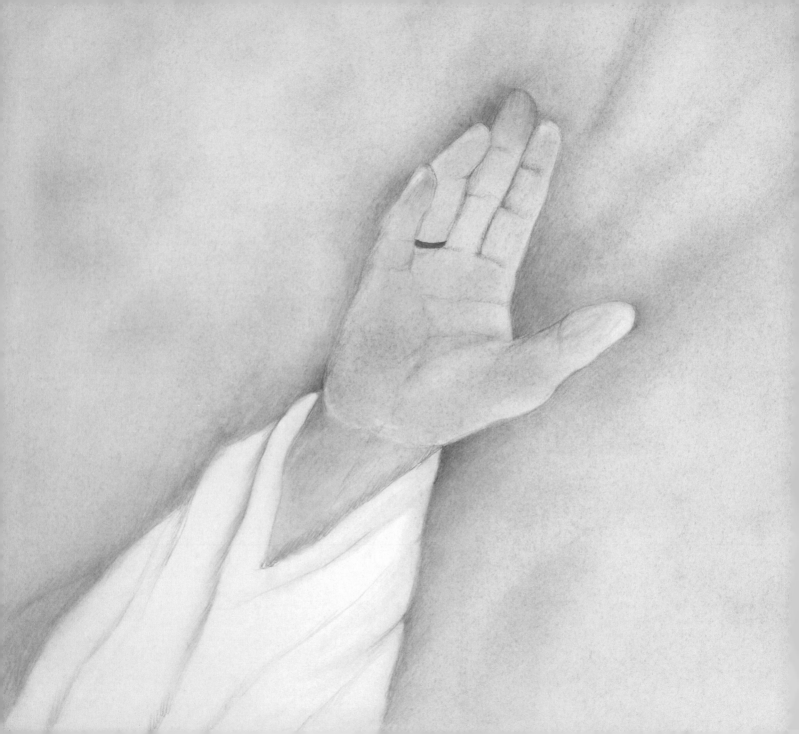

It was to be their last goodbye, but Jacob knew that
he would feel this last embrace of the Pope forever.
Jacob knew he would forever feel John Paul II's
blessing of hope that we should all spread love, peace,
and friendship as best we can in our families, in our
neighborhoods, and among different religions and
people around the world. In so doing, perhaps we
will reach the dream to one day create a world that
appreciates the miracles of life. In a world
where we truly reach the best of our
human spirit, we will enjoy
heaven on earth.

Jacob and Lena walked back to the hotel silently. The stars and moon shone above. They knew that they would never forget this beautiful Shabbat evening – with their friend, the Pope.

About the author:

Jacques J.M. Shore is an attorney, specializing in federal law and government relations, in Ottawa, Canada. He is married to Donna, a family physician, and they have three daughters: Emily, Amanda and Victoria. His late father, Sigmond, and mother, Lena, survived the Holocaust.

While he has written many published articles and essays on law and public policy, *Friday Night with the Pope* is Mr. Shore's second foray into the world of children's literature. His first book, *Menorah in the Night Sky*, was awarded the "Our Choice" recognition by the Canadian Children's Book Centre.

The author and his mother, Lena, with Pope John Paul II

About the illustrator:

Amalia Hoffman exhibited widely in galleries and museums throughout the United States. Her intricate artwork has been featured in New York City's most prestigious stores where she created innovative window displays.

She is recipient of the Society of Children's Book Writers and Illustrators 2005 Portfolio Award in the category of Fantasy.

Amalia lives and works in Larchmont, New York.